Funding & Advocacy in O&P
A Pocket Guide for US Clinics and Users

Jennifer Latham Robinson, CFm

Content and Images
Copyright 2024 Jennifer Latham Robinson, CFm

All rights reserved.

ISBN: 978-1-304-11332-0

Contents

Introduction	1
What is O&P?	3
Device Basics	7
Understanding Insurance Plans	10
HCPCS Codes for O&P Devices	15
Common Administrative Roles in O&P	18
Elements of Insurance Coverage Verification	24
CMS & Its Golden Rule: The LCD	27
Recording Calls for Insurance Verification	29
Common Limitations/Exclusions	31
Telling the Story of Medical Necessity	35
Document, Document, Everywhere	37
Alternative Funding Sources	41
Ease the Burden	43
Shared Knowledge	45

Introduction

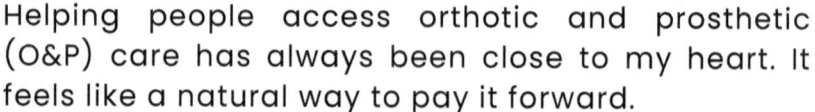

Helping people access orthotic and prosthetic (O&P) care has always been close to my heart. It feels like a natural way to pay it forward.

I was born with bilateral proximal femoral focal deficiency (PFFD), a condition that affects the hips and femurs. PFFD varies in severity, from a mild leg length difference to the complete absence of the femur. People with PFFD often use various assistive devices, such as shoe lifts, braces, prosthetic limbs, wheelchairs, crutches, or canes.

I received my first prosthetic leg when I was about two years old. I actually still have it and at this point, it's literally an antique. The way I get around has always been fluid, often combining the use of a prosthesis, crutches, and a wheelchair—a sort of mobility toolbelt. My care was provided at no charge, thanks to Shriners Children's hospital. Around the same time that I graduated out of their care, I became a professional in the O&P field. Suddenly, I gained a view behind the scenes. Not only in understanding how these devices are made, but in how they are paid for.

I began working in this field in 1999 and have experience as a technician, administrator, marketer, advocate, and owner. Over the years, I've seen the profound impact that access to O&P care can have on a person's life. But I've also seen the challenges—both financial and logistical—that can stand in the way.

This journey has fueled my passion for helping individuals navigate these obstacles and for advocating for systemic changes that make O&P care more accessible and equitable for everyone who needs it.

Through this guide, I hope to share my experiences and insights with you—whether you are a device user, practitioner, administrator, student, policymaker, or simply someone interested in understanding more about this incredible field. My goal is to provide you with the knowledge and tools needed to make a difference, just as many have made a difference in my life. Together, we can work towards a future where everyone has the opportunity to move freely, live fully, and achieve their potential.

My 'Why'
This guide is my way of sharing the knowledge and tools that have made a difference in my life, with the hope that they can help others do the same.

What is O&P?

Orthotics and Prosthetics (**O&P**) is a specialized field within the durable medical equipment (**DME**) industry, focusing on the design, fabrication, and provision of prosthetic limbs and orthopedic bracing. Depending on the clinic, additional services such as diabetic shoes, post-mastectomy supplies, and other supportive devices may also be offered. Individuals may need O&P devices for various reasons, including injury, congenital conditions, trauma, cancer, or other neuromuscular, skeletal, or circulatory issues.

Ancient Egypt saw early prosthetic care, with evidence including a wooden toe found on a mummy dating from 950–710 BCE, demonstrating that artificial limbs were used to enhance mobility long ago. The development of prosthetic limbs accelerated after wars, especially World War I and II, as the high number of amputees spurred innovations in design and materials. The urgent need to restore mobility to injured soldiers led to breakthroughs in prosthetic technology, laying the foundation for the advanced devices used today.

Despite today's incredible innovations, accessibility for everyday people remains a major challenge. This is part of a larger issue involving accessibility of all healthcare needs, not just O&P.

To see how O&P advancements impact everyday lives, it's important to examine how O&P clinics operate in the United States.

O&P providers operate under the guidance of physicians or other medical professionals, such as nurse practitioners, similar to the pharmacy industry. When a doctor prescribes medication, you take that prescription to a pharmacist to be filled. In O&P, the person seeking O&P care takes the physician prescription for the device to an O&P clinic.

Prescribing physicians also play a crucial role in documenting the medical necessity for specific O&P components, a topic we'll explore further later. Other medical professionals, such as wound care doctors and physical therapists, also collaborate closely with O&P providers.

O&P integrates science, art, and psychology to address the unique needs of individuals. Some individuals require these devices for a short term, while others may need them long-term or for life.

O&P clinical roles, and their focus, include:

>**Orthotists**: orthotic bracing
>**Prosthetists**: prosthetic limbs
>**Pedorthists**: foot care (below the ankle)
>**Fitters**: non-custom supplies and devices
>**Assistants**: support clinical team
>**Residents**: clinicians in training

As technologies evolve, more O&P clinics are adding other specialists to their clinical team. For example, having a digital engineer on staff is becoming more common.

Many O&P practitioners specialize in more than one area. It's common for a practitioner to be both an orthotist and prosthetist (referred to as a certified prosthetist/orthotist, or CPO).

An advanced post-graduate degree is required in order to become an orthotist or prosthetist. After graduation, residents must gain clinical experience and obtain special certifications before they can function independently.

Unlike orthotists and prosthetists, who require advanced degrees and certification, other clinical roles only require certification programs without the need for an advanced post-graduate degree.

Ensuring that clinicians are properly qualified and certified is essential for providing quality care. Two main certifying organizations maintain and list the certification status of all qualified clinicians:

The American Board for Certification in Orthotics, Prosthetics & Pedorthics (**ABC**)
https://www.abcop.org

Board of Certification/Accreditation (**BOC**)
https://bocusa.org

Along with clinicians, dedicated support staff members play a crucial role in ensuring comprehensive care and quality service in O&P clinics.

Technicians, who also have the opportunity to become certified, fabricate the devices and can perform major adjustments during device users' visits at the O&P clinic. Sometimes technicians are responsible for ordering components and materials, though it's also common to have a separate purchasing agent assigned to those tasks.

Each O&P clinic may have slightly different staff structures, services, and processes. For example, larger clinics often have more compartmentalized roles while staff in very small clinics might wear multiple hats. Either way, it takes a village to produce these devices and provide users with positive experiences with great outcomes. Speaking of the devices...

Let's start by exploring the main elements of O&P devices, then we can dig into how they are paid for.

Did you know?
An O&P clinic can be a privately owned local clinic, a privately owned business with multiple locations across many states, or part of a national public company.

If device users are looking for a prosthetist, the **Amputee Coalition** has a great on tool its website called 'The Prosthetist Finder'. Simply enter the zip code and it will provide a list of certified professionals in the area.
https://www.amputee-coalition.org

Device Basics

Orthotic Bracing

Orthotic bracing supports various body parts and comes in three categories: **"off-the-shelf**,**" "custom-fitted**,**"** and **"custom-fabricated**.**"** "Off-the-shelf" braces, such as those for the ankle, are available at pharmacies and do not necessarily require professional fitting, though consulting a specialist can ensure the device is appropriate. "Custom-fitted" orthotics involve significant adjustments by a professional to achieve the proper fit. "Custom-fabricated" orthotics are made from a mold or scan of the user's body and are crafted from scratch. These devices can be made from various materials, including heat-molded plastics, 3D-printed plastics, carbon fiber, metal, leather, fabric, and silicone. Orthotic devices address a range of needs, from head to toe, including helmets, spinal support, and limb bracing.

Prosthetic Limbs

A custom-fabricated limb prosthesis typically includes two major components: the **socket** and the attached components. The socket is the part that fits over the residual limb and is created from a mold or digital scan of the body. It is designed to relieve pressure on sensitive areas, like bony prominences, while providing support for weight-bearing areas. Various socket designs and suspension systems are used to secure the prosthesis to the body. The socket often needs replacement if the shape or size of the residual limb changes. Supplies, such as socks and liners, are replaced periodically throughout the year.

Components like elbows, hands, knees, and feet are attached to the prosthetic socket. Until you are involved in the prosthetic world, it can be difficult to appreciate the vast range of options available. Manufacturers operate on a global scale, much like car manufacturers, with each component offering unique features, benefits, and drawbacks. Lower extremity components are designed to accommodate specific body weights and activity levels. They may be either mechanical or computerized.

During the evaluation process, a prosthetist will have a detailed discussion to understand the user's needs and goals. For example, a user who plays golf might benefit from a foot that provides extra torsion for an improved swing.

As there is so much information available online and in print, users can research their options, but the prosthetist will ultimately guide the choice based on the user's anatomy, weight, activity level, and overall prosthetic design. It's also important to consider that insurance coverage guidelines often have specific rules for components, which can affect available options. Many users have the opportunity to trial a component before making a permanent decision.

Components are typically replaced due to irreparable damage or changing user needs.

Both orthotic and prosthetic devices are defined by the body part they involve. For instance:

Ankle-Foot-Orthosis (**AFO**)
Transtibial Prosthesis (below-knee, **BK**)
Transradial Prosthesis (below-the-elbow, **BE**)

An **endoskeletal** prosthesis has an internal mechanical structure, like a mechanical skeleton, that is sometimes covered by an outer shell. An **exoskeletal** prosthesis, on the other hand, lacks an internal mechanical structure. This design was more common in older prosthetic designs, where the internal components and outer shell are one. It may be hard to imagine, but prosthetic limbs were carved out of wood in the olden days.

Prosthetic limbs can be designed to look realistic, with basic skin-colored coverings, or to stand out with bright colors and bold, custom designs. It's important to ensure that device users have a say in how their devices look, as they are the ones who wear them every day.

It's worth noting that most insurance plans limit coverage for highly realistic limb prostheses. For detailed realism, including custom skin texture and painting, most users must seek alternative funding.

Understanding Insurance Plans

Navigating insurance coverage for orthotics and prosthetics can be complex due to the variety of insurance plans available, each with its own set of rules and coverage options. From federal programs like Medicare and Medicaid to private commercial and employer-sponsored plans, understanding what each plan covers is crucial for managing both care and costs. Additionally, plans available through the ACA Marketplace, individual insurance policies, and VA benefits offer different levels of coverage and requirements. In this section, we'll break down the specifics of these various insurance options to help you understand how to navigate their coverage guidelines.

Medicare: Medicare is a federal program primarily for individuals aged 65 and older, as well as some younger people with disabilities. Medicare Part B covers certain prosthetic devices and orthotics, such as prosthetic limbs and braces, when deemed medically necessary. Coverage specifics can vary, so it's important to review the details of the coverage guidelines.

Medicare Advantage Plans: Also known as Medicare Part C, these are alternative ways to receive Medicare benefits. Offered by private insurance companies approved by Medicare, they provide the same coverage as Traditional Medicare (Parts A and B) but often come with additional benefits, such as prescription drug coverage, dental, vision, hearing, and wellness programs.

Some Medicare Advantage plans have gained a reputation for imposing greater O&P restrictions compared to Traditional Medicare, as well as delaying care due to lengthy authorization processes. Fortunately, new legislation has been passed that requires Medicare Advantage plans to provide coverage aligning with Traditional Medicare's guidelines.

Medicaid: Medicaid is a joint federal and state program providing health coverage for low-income individuals and families. Coverage for orthotics and prosthetics can vary by state but generally includes many essential devices and services. Each state sets its own rules and limitations, so it's crucial to check the specific Medicaid plan details.

Commercial Plans: These private health insurance plans can vary widely in coverage for orthotics and prosthetics. Commercial plans often have different levels of coverage, requirements, and limitations. Reviewing the individual plan is key to understanding what is covered and any potential out-of-pocket costs.

Employer-Sponsored Plans: Offered through an employer, these plans usually provide a range of coverage, often including orthotics and prosthetics. The extent of coverage and associated costs can vary depending on the employer's plan and the insurance provider.

ACA Plans: Plans available through the Affordable Care Act (ACA) Marketplace must cover essential health benefits, which include some orthotics and prosthetics. These plans are required to meet certain standards but can vary in terms of coverage specifics and costs. Reviewing plan details is important to understand the coverage provided.

VA Benefits: For Veterans, the Department of Veterans Affairs (VA) provides coverage for prosthetics and orthotics through its benefits program. This can include a range of devices and services related to limb loss or mobility issues. Eligibility and coverage details are based on individual service records and needs.

Individual Insurance Plans (Non-ACA): These are health insurance plans purchased directly from insurance companies outside of the ACA Marketplace. Coverage for orthotics and prosthetics in these plans can be highly variable and sometimes restrictive. Some individual plans may have limited or specific criteria for coverage, including higher out-of-pocket costs or stricter eligibility requirements. Reviewing the specific details of these plans is essential to understand what is covered and what is not.

Workers' Compensation: Workers' Compensation is a type of insurance that provides benefits to employees who experience work-related injuries or illnesses. If someone is injured on the job and requires orthotic or prosthetic devices as part of the treatment, Workers' Compensation may cover the cost. Coverage typically includes medical care, rehabilitation services, and the necessary orthotic or prosthetic devices needed for recovery and return to work. The specifics of what is covered can vary by state and employer, but Workers' Compensation is designed to ensure that employees receive the medical support they need without bearing the financial burden themselves.

Auto-Insurance: Coverage for orthotic and prosthetic (O&P) devices through auto insurance can vary significantly based on the policy and the state. While some auto insurance policies may cover these devices if they are medically necessary due to injuries sustained in a car accident, there are often coverage limits that may not fully cover the cost of the device. This can result in coverage gaps, leaving individuals responsible for substantial out-of-pocket expenses.

It's important to determine whether the need for an O&P device is related to a work-related injury or a car accident. In cases of third-party liability, Medicare or other insurance companies may refuse to accept financial responsibility for the device, expecting the third party to cover the costs. Additionally, researching set-asides is crucial for long-term device coverage, as these funds are often designated to cover future medical expenses related to the injury, ensuring that the individual continues to receive necessary care without financial gaps.

Each type of payer, and individual plans, have their own set of rules and coverage options, so it's important to carefully review the specifics to ensure that orthotic and prosthetic devices are covered appropriately. Understanding the nuances of each plan can help in planning and managing the costs associated with these essential devices.

Choose Wisely!

Sometimes, people have limited options when it comes to choosing an insurance plan. Typically, plans with the largest networks tend to be more expensive. When selecting a plan, it's important to check if your essential medical care providers are in-network. Additionally, some plans may offer a 'single case agreement,' allowing out-of-network providers to be covered at in-network rates if no in-network provider is available within a certain distance.

There's a lot to consider when choosing an insurance plan. O&P clinic administrators should be careful when offering insurance advice to prosthetic users, as coverage for all medical care, not just O&P devices, needs to be considered. However, administrators can certainly answer questions and lend support in this decision-making process.

HCPCS Codes for O&P Devices

In the world of orthotic and prosthetic care, HCPCS codes play a crucial role in determining coverage and reimbursement for various devices. HCPCS, which stands for Healthcare Common Procedure Coding System, is a set of codes used to describe specific medical services and products. For orthotics and prosthetics, these codes provide a standardized way to identify and bill for different types of devices and components.

Each orthotic or prosthetic component is assigned a unique HCPCS code, which helps insurance companies and healthcare providers communicate about the device and its associated costs. These codes are essential for understanding what is covered under a specific insurance plan and can significantly impact reimbursement and out-of-pocket costs.

To fully understand coverage for a device, it is important to check the specific HCPCS code assigned to that device. For example, a microprocessor knee, often coded with L5856, may have different coverage criteria compared to a non-computerized knee unit. Insurance plans have distinct requirements and reimbursement rates for each HCPCS code, reflecting differences in technology, complexity, and cost.

In the context of prosthetics and orthotics, HCPCS codes are divided into two main categories: 'base' codes and 'addition' codes.

'Base' Codes

The 'base' code refers to the main code that describes the type of prosthesis or orthotic device being provided. For instance, there are specific 'base' codes for different types of prostheses, such as:

- Below-the-Knee (BK) Endoskeletal Prosthesis
- Above-the-Knee (AK) Endoskeletal Prosthesis
- Myoelectric Below-Elbow Prosthesis
- BK and AK Socket Replacements

These 'base' codes are the foundation for billing and represent the primary device being delivered to the individual.

'Addition' Codes

'Addition' codes are used to bill for the various components and features that are added to the 'base' code for the prosthetic or orthotic device. These might include components like a microprocessor knee, specialized foot, or additional straps and locks. Each of these components has its own HCPCS 'addition' code, which is billed alongside the 'base' code to reflect the complete configuration of the device.

For example, if an individual is receiving a below-knee (transtibial) prosthesis with a dynamic response foot and a vacuum-assisted suspension system, each of these components would have its own 'addition' code. The combination of the 'base' code and the relevant 'addition' codes gives a complete picture of the device provided to that person.

Supplies and Individual Items
Some items, like liners, socks, or maintenance supplies, do not need to be billed with a 'base' code. These items can be billed individually using their specific HCPCS codes, as they are considered separate from the primary prosthetic or orthotic device.

'Unlisted' Codes
Rarely, there is no standard HCPCS code for a device or component. In that case, providers may use an 'unlisted' code with a narrative description of what the device or component is. 'Unlisted' codes do not have associated allowables or pricing, so it's usually necessary to prove the reasoning behind the charge associated with the code. Manufacturer invoices and a breakdown of labor are often used to justify charges for 'unlisted' procedure codes. Insurance reimbursement for 'unlisted' codes can vary and are sometimes difficult to predict.

Date of Service
The date of service for an O&P device is the day that the user takes the device home. The billing for HCPCS codes includes all the appointments and work done to order, fabricate, and deliver the device. For 90 days after delivery, it is the provider's responsibility to perform routine adjustments and maintenance at no charge. Signing for delivery acknowledges that the prosthetic user is happy with the outcome. Insurance and authorizations, if applicable, need to be effective on the date of service. If changes to coverage are known prior to delivery, additional authorization efforts can be made.

Common Administrative Roles in O&P

Administrative roles in O&P clinics play a crucial role in supporting device users. Unlike clinical positions, many newly hired administrative professionals in this field lack specialized training tailored to O&P. In this section, we will break down the responsibilities of common administrative roles and explore how these professionals interact with and support device users, ensuring they have a seamless and positive experience throughout their care journey.

Front Desk/In-Take
The Front Desk/In-Take role is key to shaping the user's experience at an O&P clinic. This person interacts with users by answering calls, scheduling appointments, receiving faxes, and managing patient data. Initial online insurance verification is often completed at check-in, giving a preliminary check on insurance status, while a more thorough benefit review follows the evaluation.

This role needs someone who's friendly and easy to talk to since they'll be the first person users interact with. Good communication is key to making sure people feel understood and cared for, even when things get hectic. Juggling tasks like answering calls, helping people in person, scheduling, checking insurance, and entering data takes solid organizational skills and the ability to figure out what's most important. Being adaptable and staying upbeat are vital for keeping things running smoothly and making sure every user has a good experience.

The Authorizations/Referral Specialist

This role plays a vital part in navigating the complexities of insurance coverage to ensure users receive the devices they need. This person carefully reviews insurance policies, identifies coverage gaps, and ensures all necessary paperwork is completed. They also scrutinize documentation from prosthetists and orthotists to support device requests effectively.

In interactions with users, this administrator provides crucial support by explaining coverage details, addressing concerns, and managing the authorization process. Once authorization is obtained, clinical staff must be quickly informed.

Care Coordinator

The Care Coordinator is essential for guiding individuals through the entire fitting process, ensuring they feel consistently supported. This role demands a natural empathy and strong communication skills, as it involves interacting with users, physicians, clinicians, and other team members.

The Care Coordinator ensures that everyone involved in a user's care is aligned, managing details and staying proactive to prevent issues. Acting as the central point of contact, they help create a seamless, coordinated experience from start to finish, making sure users receive the comprehensive support they need throughout their journey. Additionally, they ensure that each case in progress has a clear plan for future actions, keeping the process on track and moving forward.

Biller

The Biller is crucial in ensuring that insurance claims are accurate before submission and managing the entire submission process. This role is ideal for someone detail-oriented who thrives behind the scenes, meticulously reviewing claims and catching any errors to ensure all information is correct.

A great Biller needs a solid understanding of insurance processes and the ability to navigate complex policies and requirements. They must be organized and methodical, managing deadlines and tracking multiple claims simultaneously. Additionally, the Biller ensures that each claim has a clear path to resolution, keeping the billing process smooth and efficient for users and the clinic alike.

Accounts Receivable (A/R)

The Accounts Receivable (A/R) role in an O&P clinic is key to managing incoming payments and resolving payment issues. Ideal for someone organized and persistent, this role involves tracking payments, following up on unpaid claims, and handling insurance denials.

The A/R specialist must be detail-oriented, adept at insurance appeals, and able to communicate effectively with insurance companies. Patience and a methodical approach are essential, as resolving payment issues can be slow. They also ensure each case has a clear plan for follow-up, keeping the clinic's finances on track. Their efforts help maintain financial stability and ensure that the clinic can continue to provide quality care.

Accounts Payable (AP)

Accounts Payable (AP) is responsible for managing the O&P clinic's bills, handling invoices, and maintaining accurate financial records. This role is often filled by an accountant, either on-site or off-site, whose expertise in financial management ensures timely payments, proper fund allocation, and good vendor relationships. The ideal person for this role is detail-oriented, organized, and skilled in budgeting and compliance, playing a crucial part in the clinic's financial stability and smooth operation.

Human Resources (HR)

Human Resources (HR) in an O&P clinic is responsible for managing employee relations, hiring, benefits administration, and ensuring compliance with labor laws. This role might be handled by an in-house HR professional or outsourced to an external agency. The best person for this role is someone who is skilled in communication, organized, and knowledgeable about both HR practices and the unique needs of a healthcare environment. Whether on-site or through an outside agency, effective HR management is essential for maintaining a positive workplace culture and supporting the clinic's staff.

Marketing

The Marketing role in an O&P clinic is multifaceted and can vary greatly depending on the size of the clinic. This role is essential for developing and implementing marketing strategies, identifying potential clients, and maintaining relationships

In smaller to midsize clinics, this role often includes managing social media, creating online content, and conducting direct outreach to individuals needing O&P devices. Larger O&P clinics may have a separate person handling some of these tasks, particularly social media.

A successful O&P marketer connects with people, building trust through authentic communication. They need to understand the needs of referral sources and patients, helping the clinic adapt its services to meet those needs. Creativity and strategic thinking are key, especially when managing multiple marketing channels. By identifying and engaging with the community, the marketer plays a crucial role in driving the clinic's growth and promoting a positive presence for the team.

Interconnected Roles
In many O&P clinics, the **Office Manager** supervises administrative staff and may also take on tasks such as billing or accounts payable. In smaller clinics, it's common for roles to often overlap, such as a biller also managing accounts receivable.

Understanding how these roles connect and the benefits of cross-training is important for new administrative staff. Cross-training helps everyone see how their work affects the whole team and improves the overall experience for users.

This teamwork ensures that every part of a user's journey, from the first contact to billing, runs smoothly and efficiently.

Staff Members Who Are Device Users

In any role within an O&P clinic, having staff with a personal connection to orthotics and prosthetics—whether through personal use of a device or through a close relationship with someone who does—can significantly enhance the quality of service provided. This personal connection brings a deeper level of understanding and empathy, allowing staff to relate to device users' experiences on a more meaningful level. Such staff can offer valuable insights and support, helping to build stronger, more compassionate relationships with customers. Their firsthand knowledge can also improve communication and problem-solving, as they are better equipped to anticipate and address people's needs and concerns. While not a necessity, this depth of personal connection can greatly enrich the device user's experience, making interactions more genuine and supportive.

True, having device users on staff is wonderful. Peer support for people new to limb loss has become a standard of care for O&P clinics. This provides an opportunity for someone experienced as a prosthetic user to offer support and encouragement to those new to the process. The Amputee Coalition offers **Certified Peer Visitors (CPVs)** who have been trained for this role. CPVs provide an unbiased and trained approach to support and can be located by contacting the Amputee Coalition directly. CPVs, along with device users on staff, can make a profound impact on the emotional well-being of people new to limb loss.

Elements of Insurance Coverage Verification

Understanding administrative roles helps clarify how each function supports a smooth user experience. A key part of this process is insurance benefit verification, which ensures coverage for devices and underscores the importance of effective coordination within the clinic.

Understanding insurance terms related to orthotics and prosthetics is crucial for both device users and professionals managing healthcare expenses. Here's a breakdown of some key concepts:

Deductible:
A deductible is the amount a person must pay out-of-pocket for covered services before insurance begins to share the costs. For example, if the deductible is $1,000, the individual will need to cover the first $1,000 of the medical expenses. Once the deductible is met, the insurance will start covering a portion of the costs according to the terms of the insurance plan.

Coinsurance:
Coinsurance is the percentage of costs a person pays for covered services after meeting the deductible. For instance, if the coinsurance is 20% and an orthotic device costs $1000, the individual would pay $200 while the insurance covers the remaining $800. Coinsurance rates vary depending on the insurance plan and are typically applied to most covered O&P services.

Out-of-Pocket Maximum:
The out-of-pocket maximum is the highest amount a person will have to pay for covered services in a plan year. After reaching this limit, the insurance will cover 100% of the costs for covered services for the remainder of the year. This maximum includes deductibles, coinsurance, and co-payments, but usually does not cover premiums or costs for services not included in the plan.

In/Out of Network Coverage:
In-network coverage applies to services provided by healthcare providers who have agreements with an insurance company. Using in-network providers generally means lower costs due to negotiated discounted rates. Out-of-network coverage refers to services from providers who are not part of the insurance network.

In some cases, out-of-network services may not be covered at all. If they are covered, coinsurance rates will typically be higher because they are based on the full, non-discounted rates of the provider.

Authorization Requirements:
Authorization involves getting approval from an insurance company before certain services or devices are covered. For orthotics and prosthetics, this usually means obtaining pre-authorization, which involves submitting documentation to confirm that the device is medically necessary and meets the insurance company's criteria. Without proper authorization, insurance may deny coverage or reduce the amount they pay.

Being familiar with these insurance terms helps both device users and professionals manage the costs associated with orthotics and prosthetics.

It's important to review insurance policy details and communicate with insurance providers to ensure a clear understanding of coverage and the device user's out-of-pocket expenses. Every effort should be made to inform the user of potential financial responsibilities prior to ordering or fabrication.

Usual & Customary Rate (U&C) vs. Allowable Rate:
The usual and customary rate (U&C) is the standard rate a clinic charges for each HCPCS code. The allowable rate is the discounted rate agreed upon between the clinic and the payer source.

If an O&P clinic is an 'in-network' or 'participating' provider, the device user is not responsible for the difference between the U&C charge and the allowable rate.

Example:

A usual and customary charge for a HCPCS code is $100. The individual's responsibility is 20%. If the O&P clinic is in-network with the individual's insurance company, and the agreed-upon amount (or discounted amount) is $80, the device user would owe 20% of $80 (excluding any deductible).

The difference between the $100 (U&C) and $80 (allowed) would be adjusted as a contractual adjustment.

CMS & Its Golden Rule: The LCD

When navigating insurance coverage for orthotic and prosthetic devices, we should understand the role of the Centers for Medicare & Medicaid Services (CMS) and Medicare. CMS is the federal agency that oversees Medicare, Medicaid, and other health programs. While Medicare is a specific program under CMS that provides health coverage mainly to individuals aged 65 and older, as well as some younger people with disabilities, CMS sets the broader policies and guidelines that influence how these programs operate.

One essential resource provided by CMS is the Local Coverage Determination (LCD). The LCD is a document that lists all active HCPCS (Healthcare Common Procedure Coding System) codes used in orthotics and prosthetics, along with the associated documentation and billing rules. The LCD serves as a guide for determining what is covered under Medicare and helps ensure that billing practices are consistent and accurate.

You can find the current LCD on the CMS website at **www.cms.gov**. While individual insurance plans may have their own criteria and rules that differ from what's found in the LCD, the LCD is a fantastic place to start. It provides a solid foundation for understanding the coverage and billing requirements for O&P devices and certainly influences any insurance company that follows

Medicare guidelines.

So, when you're dealing with insurance coverage for O&P devices, checking the LCD can help you understand what's covered and what documentation is needed. Just keep in mind that other insurance plans might have different rules, so it's always a good idea to verify with the specific insurance provider.

By understanding HCPCS codes and detailed policy guidelines, both device users and professionals can gain insight into what is covered, any potential authorization requirements, and the associated costs. This ensures that all parties are on the same page regarding the device's coverage and helps in navigating the financial aspects of obtaining the necessary orthotic or prosthetic care.

What's in the LCD?
- Medicare coverage overview
- Documentation requirements
- HCPCS coding
- Coverage criteria
- Periodic review and updates.
- Eligibility coverage conditions
- Special considerations and policy references.

Recording Calls for Insurance Verification

When dealing with insurance for orthotics and prosthetics, accurately documenting phone conversations with insurance representatives is essential for managing coverage and claims effectively. Here's a brief guide on how to record these calls properly:

Obtain the Representative's Name: Start by noting the full name of the insurance representative you are speaking with. Sometimes only the initial of the last name is provided, so be sure to record whatever details you receive. This helps in tracking and following up on the information provided.

Record the Date and Time: Document the exact date and time of the call. This information is crucial for referencing the conversation and verifying details later.

Ask for a Call Reference Number: Request a call reference number or case number from the representative. Write it down if provided. This number can be useful for tracking the status of the inquiry or claim. If a reference number is not given, having the representative's name and the time of the call becomes even more important.

Summarize Key Details: After the call, take a moment to summarize the key points discussed, including coverage details, authorization requirements, and any next steps or actions agreed upon.

By following these steps, you create a reliable record that can be referred to in future interactions with the insurance company, ensuring consistency and clarity in managing orthotic and prosthetic care.

No matter what an insurance representative tells you over the phone, neither information nor authorizations guarantee coverage and payment. The most reliable guide is the actual benefit plan document, which outlines in writing what is covered and under what conditions. This document will also list any exclusions for specific components.

However, obtaining this document can sometimes be challenging.

For employer-sponsored plans, contacting the Human Resources (HR) department is usually the best way to get the written benefit plan document. For commercial plans, calling the insurance company's customer service can direct you to the document.

If the written plan document labels a component as 'investigational', 'experimental', or not 'medically necessary,' securing coverage may be difficult. Still, it's not always impossible. In the case of a 'self-funded' employer-sponsored plan, the employer might have the authority to override exclusions on a case-by-case basis.

The key takeaway is to verify coverage with the written plan document rather than relying solely on verbal assurances from insurance representatives.

Common Limitations/Exclusions

Frequency Exclusions
Some insurance companies impose limits on how often O&P devices can be replaced. For example, Medicare generally limits the replacement of orthotic devices to once every five years, allowing exceptions only in specific cases, such as significant changes in a device-user's condition that require a different type of brace. Similarly, some commercial insurance plans have their own frequency limits, which can often feel arbitrary.

When an exception to these limits exists—such as in cases of a change in the device-user's condition—it is crucial for the O&P clinic and prescribing physician to thoroughly document the changes in the person's anatomy and explain how the new, differently designed device will meet those needs.

Frequency limitations are most commonly applied to orthotic devices rather than prosthetics. While it's not unheard of for these restrictions to apply to prosthetic devices, it is less common.

'Experimental or Investigational'
Insurance companies sometimes label certain orthotic and prosthetic components as 'experimental' or 'investigational', meaning they consider these devices unproven or lacking sufficient evidence to be deemed medically necessary. When this happens, it's important to refer to the individual's benefit plan booklet for specific details, as there may be exceptions or

appeal options, particularly in self-insured employer-sponsored policies, which often have more flexibility in determining coverage criteria.

One effective strategy to challenge this classification is to provide the individual with a trial of the component. If the clinic and prescribing physician can document significant and measurable benefits during the trial, this evidence can be used to argue that the component should not be considered experimental or investigational. Additionally, citing recent studies, clinical guidelines, or expert opinions that support the component's efficacy may strengthen the case. Advocating for coverage often requires persistence, detailed documentation, and sometimes collaboration with the insurance provider to demonstrate that the component meets the medical necessity criteria. In the case of self-insured plans, there may be more room to negotiate these exceptions directly with the employer or plan administrator.

Custom Prosthetic Realism
As mentioned earlier, there is a psychological aspect to prosthetic rehabilitation that involves users emotionally accepting a prosthesis as part of their lives. The appearance of the prosthesis can play a crucial role in this process, whether the user desires it to look realistic or prefers a more distinctive design. Unfortunately, most funding sources do not cover hyper realistic prostheses, with exceptions possibly being the VA or Workers' Compensation. We should work together to challenge these misguided coverage policies.

Coding Combination Limits
Most pay sources limit the combinations of components that can be used. For example, many high-activity prosthetic feet are not permitted as additions for initial prostheses when they are coded as such. The reasoning behind this limitation is that an initial prosthesis is meant primarily for initial gait training. More advanced components are generally considered only after the device user has increased in their activity level and the initial prosthesis no longer meets their functional needs

Activity-Specific O&P Devices
Examples of activity-specific O&P devices include 'running' legs (with blade feet often used by Paralympians), 'swim' limbs, and 'bike' limbs. Unfortunately, the vast majority of pay sources do not consider activity-specific devices to be medically necessary. The 'So Every BODY Can Move' (SEBCM) movement is a national effort pushing for legislation in each state to ensure insurance coverage for these devices. Coverage for activity-specific O&P devices is more commonly considered by Workers' Compensation or the VA.

It should be noted that the provision of activity-specific devices can greatly enhance the mental and physical well-being of people living with limb loss and limb difference. As the SEBCM slogan states, 'Movement is medicine,' and it can actually reduce overall healthcare costs associated with obesity, mental health challenges, and diabetes.
https://soeverybodycanmove.org

Back-Up Devices

Another frustrating limitation is the lack of coverage for 'back-up' devices. 'Back-up' devices can be incredibly important in the event that the primary device becomes unusable, such as when a device is irreparably damaged. Custom devices take time to fabricate, so a 'back-up' device can ensure that the user maintains the ability to perform everyday living activities.

Coverage for 'back-up' O&P devices is more commonly considered by Workers' Compensation.

Lifecare Plans

Life care plans often play a significant role in Workers' Compensation settlements, where the Workers' Compensation company projects the costs associated with an injured worker's needs over their lifetime. It's crucial to account for the replacement of devices every few years to address anatomical changes, evolving functional needs, and potential irreparable damage. Clinics can play an important role by providing replacement timelines and cost estimates that align with the user's care plan and goals. If possible, the inclusion of 'backup' devices and 'activity-specific' devices should also be considered.

Telling the Story of Medical Necessity

In a nutshell, the medical necessity of an O&P device and/or specific component answers these key questions:

What is a day-in-the-life of the potential device user? This includes identifying environmental barriers and the specific actions the individual must perform in their home and community. This information should be incredibly specific and unique to that person—avoid using templates.

How will the specific device/component meet those unique needs? Here, directly relate the features of the device to the needs identified in the first question, showing how it addresses the person's specific challenges.

If an existing device is being replaced, how does the current specific device/component fail to meet the person's unique needs, and how will the proposed device/component better fulfill those needs? Again, specificity is crucial.

There are only a few insurance-approved reasons for replacing an existing device, and additional limitations on replacement frequency may apply, depending on the pay source. The most common justifications, according to most insurance companies, include irreparable damage not covered under warranty or a change in the person's condition, anatomy, or functional needs.

The pay source's detailed plan document will provide specific replacement criteria.

Why describe this process as 'telling the story'? Often, a person may not immediately realize that their functional level has increased. It might take a conversation for them to recognize, "Wow, I'm actually doing a lot more now than when I first received my initial prosthesis. And, yes, these current components are holding me back from reaching my potential." Any request for a replacement device should be framed within the context of a change between two points in time: (a) when the current device/component was received and (b) when the change occurred.

A Device User's Guide to Physician Appointments

If a device user is having trouble with their current device, it's a good idea to book an appointment with the O&P clinic before seeing a physician. While it's technically a follow-up, this visit is a great chance to figure out exactly what's wrong and what needs to be done to fix it. If a major part needs replacing, physician notes will be needed to explain the situation in detail. Users can ask the O&P clinic for a 'Dear Doctor' letter that lays out what's needed and why. It's also important for physicians to document any environmental challenges and daily activities. Since most insurance companies require recent physician notes, it's also smart to bring this up even during yearly wellness exams.

Document, Document, Everywhere

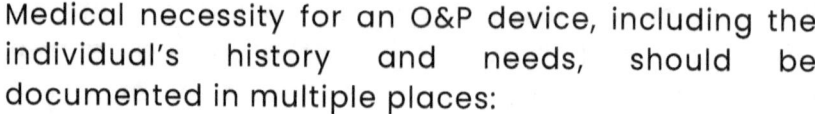

Medical necessity for an O&P device, including the individual's history and needs, should be documented in multiple places:

Physician Note: For O&P devices, a physician (or anyone eligible to prescribe O&P devices, per the LCD) must not only prescribe the device, but also include specific details about the medical necessity in their recent notes.

Sometimes, physicians are asked to document information that might be outside their usual expertise. For instance, a primary care physician may struggle to document the need for a high-tech prosthetic component because they may not be familiar with the specific details required. To address this, many clinics refer patients to specialists in rehabilitation, like PM&R doctors (physiatrists). These specialists are trained to handle complex cases involving spinal cord injuries, brain injuries, strokes, amputations, and chronic pain. They focus on restoring function and improving quality of life through treatments such as physical therapy, medications, and assistive devices, often working with a team of professionals.

With the current acceptance of telehealth notes for documenting O&P device needs, many clinics use this opportunity to ensure they get the necessary physician documentation. The best way to ensure physicians know what's being asked of them is for O&P clinics to provide their notes and recommendations before the physicians evaluate the individual, when possible.

This is most relevant when an individual currently using a device returns to the O&P clinic for a follow-up. During this appointment, the O&P clinician may determine that a new device is needed. In such cases, the individual must return to a physician to discuss the need and obtain the required documentation. O&P administrative staff often send 'Dear Doctor' letters, which provide all the necessary information and the O&P provider's input to meet the documentation needs of a specific payer.

These 'Dear Doctor' letters do not instruct the physician on exactly what to write but rather educate them on the key points that need to be addressed according to insurance requirements, while also providing the O&P clinic's perspective. Otherwise, the physician may not know what to document, leading the O&P clinic to request an amended encounter note later. Amended notes are not only inconvenient for physicians, but there are also limitations on when and how an encounter note can be amended.

O&P Clinician Note: The O&P clinician is responsible for documenting a thorough history of the individual, including subjective information, objective information, assessments, and plan. This is referred to as a 'SOAP' note. These categories of information include detailed descriptions such as anatomy, functional level assessments, descriptions of activities, and the justification for all components of the recommended device.

Subjective Information:
This includes the individual's reported experiences, symptoms, and personal account of their condition and functional challenges.

Objective Information:
This encompasses measurable data collected during the assessment, such as physical examination findings, test results, and observations of the individual's functional abilities.

Assessment:
This section provides a professional evaluation of the individual's needs based on the subjective and objective information, including any diagnosis or identification of issues that the O&P device will address.

Plan:
This outlines the proposed course of action, including the specific O&P device components recommended, the rationale for their selection, and the goals for the intervention.

The 'SOAP' note should be detailed and specific, capturing the individual's unique needs and justifying the chosen components of the recommended device.

This thorough documentation supports the medical necessity and facilitates communication with insurance providers, ensuring that the individual receives the appropriate coverage and care.

Additional provider notes, such as those from a physical therapist, might sometimes be recommended, particularly for advanced computerized components.

Pulling all of these puzzle pieces together requires significant effort, including phone calls, emails, faxes, and more.

If It's Not Written, It Didn't Happen
In the field of orthotics and prosthetics, documenting all communications—whether with insurance companies, referring providers, or people in need of O&P devices—is crucial. Thorough documentation ensures there is a clear record of conversations, decisions, and agreements, which can be vital for resolving disputes, securing reimbursements, and ensuring continuity of care. Detailed records help protect everyone, by providing evidence of due diligence and supporting the delivery of high-quality care. In essence, if it's not documented, it's as if it didn't happen, making meticulous record-keeping an essential practice.

O&P Medical Records
Most O&P clinics use electronic medical record (**EMR**) systems that are specifically designed for the O&P field. There are a few major O&P EMR systems available today. While they may operate differently, they all share the goal of creating a paperless medical record.

Alternative Funding Sources

When exploring funding sources for orthotics and prosthetic devices, several additional avenues beyond traditional insurance can offer support. Here are just a few examples of alternative funding sources:

Vocational Rehabilitation:
Vocational Rehabilitation (VR) programs provide support for individuals with disabilities to help them gain and maintain employment. Many VR programs offer financial assistance for prosthetics and orthotics as part of their broader mission to improve job prospects and workplace functionality. These programs typically require an application process, and eligibility is often based on individual needs and employment goals.
https://rsa.ed.gov/about/states

Challenged Athletes Foundation (CAF):
The Challenged Athletes Foundation focuses on providing grants to athletes with physical disabilities to help cover the costs of adaptive sports equipment, including prosthetics and orthotics. CAF supports athletes at all levels, from recreational to competitive, and aims to enhance their ability to participate in sports and physical activities. Applications are usually assessed based on the athlete's needs and goals.
https://www.challengedathletes.org

Steps of Faith:
Steps of Faith is a non-profit organization

dedicated to providing financial assistance for prosthetic limbs to those who cannot afford them. They offer support to individuals who are underinsured or uninsured, helping to cover the cost of prosthetic devices and related services. The application process typically involves demonstrating financial need and providing medical documentation.
https://www.stepsoffaithfoundation.org

Catholic Charities:
Catholic Charities provides a range of support services, including financial assistance for medical needs such as prosthetics and orthotics. Their assistance programs vary by location and can include direct financial help, referrals to other resources, or support through community partnerships. Eligibility and the application process can depend on individual circumstances and local office guidelines.
https://www.catholiccharitiesusa.org

Limbs for Life:
Limbs for Life is a non-profit organization that offers financial assistance for prosthetic limbs to individuals in need. Their mission is to help those who are unable to afford prosthetic devices. The organization typically requires an application with detailed financial and medical information to determine eligibility.
https://www.limbsforlife.org

Each of these funding sources offers a unique form of assistance and may have specific application processes and eligibility criteria.

Ease the Burden

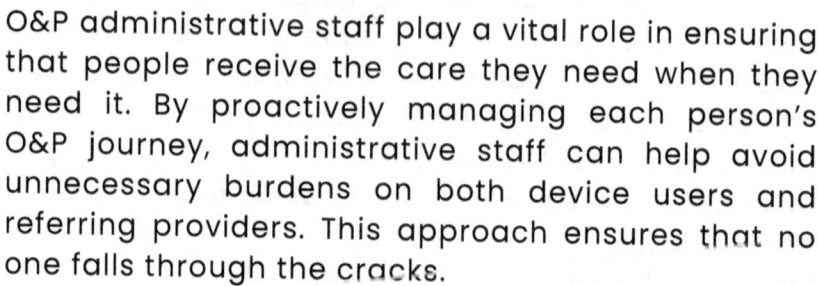

O&P administrative staff play a vital role in ensuring that people receive the care they need when they need it. By proactively managing each person's O&P journey, administrative staff can help avoid unnecessary burdens on both device users and referring providers. This approach ensures that no one falls through the cracks.

People requiring O&P devices often face significant challenges, so it's important not to wait for them to reach out, unless they've specifically requested that approach. By being proactive and supportive, administrative staff can help them navigate their care with greater ease and less stress.

Here's a list of practical ways O&P administrators can proactively help to manage each case:

- Following regularly by phone and mail to reschedule canceled or missed appointments.
- Calling individuals with updates on their authorization request.
- Following up regularly on pending documentation from referring providers.
- Keep referring professional updates on care plans.
- Collaborating with O&P clinicians to ensure a future appointment/action is always scheduled during the fabrication process.

Work-in-Progress (WIP) Meetings

Regular Work-in-Progress (WIP) meetings are crucial for efficiently managing O&P cases. These meetings, held regularly with both administrative and clinical staff, ensure that everyone remains aligned throughout the process—from the initial assessment and documentation to authorization, fabrication, and final delivery.

For WIP meetings to truly benefit the team and the device users, they must be more than just status updates. It's essential for these meetings to be engaging and positive. Admins play a pivotal role in setting this tone by fostering an atmosphere of active participation and collaboration. Rather than simply reading off case statuses, admins should come prepared to discuss each case in depth, address any issues, and strategize solutions. This proactive approach not only makes the meetings more productive but also helps to resolve problems more efficiently, saving everyone's time and increasing overall productivity.

By creating a collaborative atmosphere during WIP meetings, both administrative and clinical teams can work together effectively and help foster a positive work culture.

The frequency of Work-in-Progress (WIP) meetings can be adjusted to fit a clinic's needs, but consistency is crucial. Meeting once a week or every two weeks is typically recommended to keep cases on track and address issues promptly, ensuring effective case management and a positive user experience.

Shared Knowledge

For professionals new to the O&P field, understanding device funding and advocacy is crucial.

As a device user myself, I understand firsthand how vital it is to be informed and to advocate for one's needs. This knowledge should be accessible to everyone involved, not just those working behind the scenes. Transparency in healthcare is essential for empowering device users to make informed decisions and effectively navigate the complex process of securing the necessary funding and documentation.

By providing clear, comprehensive information to professionals and device users, I hope to bridge the gap between those who manage these tasks and those who rely on their outcomes. It's important for device users to have the same level of understanding as the professionals who guide their care.

There's always more to learn, and I'm committed to continuing to explore and share this information in future publications. My goal is to keep expanding on these topics, addressing new challenges, and fostering a more transparent and informed environment for everyone involved in the O&P field.

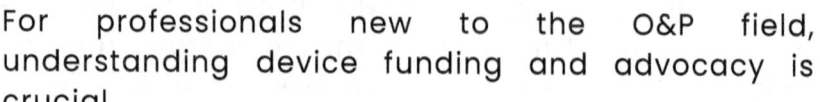

Jennifer Latham Robinson, CFm

www.ingramcontent.com/pod-product-compliance
Lightning Source LLC
Chambersburg PA
CBHW051204170526
45158CB00005B/1816